A Different

Kind of Grief

Tips for Men Going Through a Miscarriage

By: Erik Fowler

DEDICATION

This book is dedicated to my wonderfully powerful, independent and loving wife Stephanie. I couldn't imagine going through life's roller coaster ride without you.

CONTENTS

INTRODUCTION

At the time I wrote this book, in the summer of 2016, my wife Stephanie and I had recently gone through an incredibly tough and unfortunately fairly common experience of having a miscarriage. It was a very difficult time for us and we were able to get through it together as a team but it took an immense amount of effort from both of us. Stephanie and I want nothing more in life than to be parents and so to lose a child takes a real toll on both of us. It is impossible for me as a man to fully understand what Stephanie was going through when this happened to her. I had my own pain and suffering but I didn't carry this baby in my body and have the immediate chemical/physical connection that she did. Like many people I turn to books to get through difficult times and this experience was no different. I was running into a problem as I was trying to find something to read and that is a vast majority of books that I saw were for women dealing with miscarriages. In no way am I saying that is a bad thing but I just wished that there was a simple, short and straight to the point guide that laid out tips on how a man could get through this time because it is a fundamentally different experience than a woman's. So that's why I wrote this, and I hope that it can be used by men who are going through the same thing I did. It it will not cut down on the pain felt it can help the processing of emotions and help get guys through it. These are tips, not a step by step guide, and each person will be different so not every one may apply. I am also not a professional in this field, just someone who thinks my own experience can help.

IT'S NOT JUST ABOUT YOU

I quickly learned after the miscarriage happened with Stephanie is that even though I was deeply affected by it occurring it is the mother who is going through much more pain and suffering than the man. Now I am mature enough to admit the stereotype that men blow things way out of proportion when it comes to their health is mostly true. Think back to a time where you were sick and I'm sure there were times when you acted a lot sicker than you were while your partner, parent or friend was taking care of you. I am not going to discredit the heartache that the man goes through as I experienced it first-hand but this is not the time to act that way. It is important to remember that the mother carries the baby and develops a much deeper connection from the onset of the pregnancy. There are chemical and physical changes that happen and the whole "having a child" situation typically feels much more real to them at an earlier time. I too immediately felt a connection with our baby as soon as I was surprised with the news that Stephanie was expecting. I started to plan this child's life; tee-ball, trips to the museum, school plays, etc. and when we lost it I was devastated but it is important to remember that it is beyond impossible to fully know or understand exactly how the mother is feeling even if she is open with you. Stephanie did not hide any of her feelings with me, and she would try to comfort me but it is important to be her rock immediately after it happens. Basically, the point in this tip is to remember that the focus should mostly be on her and not you. Try doing things that will make her

4

happy. If there is a special dinner or snack that she loves, get it and make it for her or if it is just laying together in bed with the lights off, do that as well . I promise that you will get your time to grieve and work through these feelings but it is important to focus on the mother at first. Remember to let her know that she did nothing wrong. This was not something she could have prevented or that she caused and it is very important that she knows that.

PUMP THE BRAKES

I know in my own experience I always like to be the rock for Stephanie and I also like to be the person who likes to fix any issues that she has. I am sure most of you that are reading this book are the same way with your partner. Anything from running to the store at night if she is out of dry shampoo that she needs for work the next morning, trying to fix a stopped up drain or if she needs help with a paper for college I will do it. Most of the time this is a perfect way to act for her but at other times it can be much more of a hindrance than a help. It depends on the person and again this book is full of tips based on my own experience but sometimes the mother just needs to be sad and mourn the loss that was experienced. That is completely 100% normal. I have been found guilty of trying to find a solution to the sadness and pain that Stephanie was facing when she went through the miscarriage but it is amazing how much of a help it can be to just sit and hold her while she and often both of us just cried. No words need to be said at this moment because the physical touch and support can mean the world to her and in turn, help you. Another piece of advice that I can give is to just sit and listen to her if she needs to talk and vent. Don't say anything about how to fix the situation or how she should get through it but just listen and hear the words that she is saying, The grieving process is important for both of you though so don't forget about yourself in this step of the process. I also found it incredibly helpful to write down how I was feeling. I would write down how I was sad that this child we expected to have would not be born and I lost the opportunity to see it grow up, teach it baseball, watch school plays, etc. This will be one of the harder steps but it is important to feel sad to properly mourn and if you rush through this feeling that will never happen. Another major component of this step is to not put a time frame on the healing process. Your partner may get over the sadness step quickly in just a few days or weeks. It may also take a lot longer and that is completely ok. There is no correct time that it should take. Don't make comments if it seems to be taking her some extra time and also do not feel bad if it is taking you longer than expected to get through it.

REMEMBER TO HELP YOURSELF

As you have already read I am someone who often takes time to focus on the needs of others instead of myself and I am sure most of you are like that as well. It is a stereotypical thing that men are to support women first and not worry about themselves. I do not intend this book to be a debate on feminist issues, but I agree that it is important to be that support system only if you remember yourself in the process. This time is very hard on both of you and caring for the mother will consume a lot of your time and energy but make sure to leave some for you. I found myself wanting to just eat fast food, not work out, lay around watching Netflix and just generally do nothing. I make no arguments that there is definitely a time for that behavior, but I think that it is important to try and keep spirits as

high as they can be after the grief period and self
–care is very important. Even something as
simple as making sure you eat a piece of fruit
instead of potato chips can really make a
difference, as does getting a little bit of exercise.
Stephanie and I would go on walks which helped
in multiple ways. It gave us an opportunity to
just talk, forced us to get out of the house for a bit
and felt a little better from the exercise. Another
important tip that relates to self-care is to be
careful about missing work. It is easy to call in
sick so you can spend time at home and while
that is important to do at first it can be a slippery
slope. You do not want to run out of paid time
off , or jeopardize your career if you are taking
unpaid time. It also helps the whole situation if
you start to get into the normal routine of things
again after you properly grieve. Lastly, I would
suggest keeping your attitude in check as well. It

is easy when you are feeling sad and angry at the situation to take that out on those around you. That is the last thing that needs to happen when you are communicating with the mother. It will create unnecessary hurt feelings if you treat her poorly. A bad attitude also adds stress to yourself and that will hurt the healing process. Remember that you need to take care of yourself so you can be in a better state of mind to help your partner.

REMOVE UNNECESSARY STRESS

One you and your wife go through a miscarriage you will start to realize how much stuff you will receive as a result of it, mostly all relating to billing, insurance, etc. You will receive an explanation of benefits from the insurance company, which show how much (or little) they paid along with the benefits of your plan for the services done ad you will also mostly likely receive bills from a lot of various sources. In our own experience, we received bills from her OB/GYN, the pathologist, facility/hospital, ultrasound tech, among others. It will often turn into a mountain of paperwork to sort through it all and try to get everything paid on time but that is unnecessary stress that the mother does not need. It would be a good idea to call the hospital, doctors office, etc. and ask if they can send you one combined bill that has all the appointments and charges on it. That way you only have one bill from each provider that you need to pay instead of multiple ones for each. Some hospitals and doctors will offer the ability to autopay bills or pay by phone/online. These options make it really easy for you to take care of it and not leave it for your partner. I would also recommend to sit and think or write down other unnecessary stress's that she has and take care of them. For example, Stephanie and I share the cleaning duties for our house. We both do wash and fold laundry, load and unload the dishwasher, cook dinner, grocery shop, etc. but for the time after she had the miscarriage I took over those tasks completely so she didn't need to worry about it. It is important to let the mother know that she just needs to focus on her, instead of the little pesky tasks that have to be done since rest is so vital to her recovery. A miscarriage is a major event so if the mother needs to nap during the day help her by taking care of the house so she can. One last thing that might help in this category is to be her assistant when it comes to phone calls or visits from family. Do not tell her who she can talk to or when but just ask her when she wants to. My parents live out of town so I would ask Stephanie when she felt up to talking with them on the phone as she was recovering. I didn't want my parents to just call her when she was crying, napping or just not in the mood to talk. Just remember to give her the time and ability to heal.

DON'T FORGET THE FUTURE

One of the easiest things that someone can do in times of really tough events is to just be stuck in the present. I do feel that it is important to properly process the emotions you have and grieve but one very essential step to healing is remembering to look forward to the future. Try to just remember that the plans your partner and you have made are not completely lost. As we went through the grieving process we were able to slowly open up and start talking about our lives together and how raising a kid will be so incredibly amazing and what exactly that entailed. We were able to start our fun "arguments" about possible names again, make comments about clothes or toys we saw at stores and just start to get that hope and excitement we had before the miscarriage. We would also make suggestions about schools, or television shows they would watch and it was just a fun bonding experience. I would start to get excited again at the prospect of taking a child to the zoo, or a baseball game.   It's the hope and the security that you believe everything will be ok that will make a huge difference in this process. If you are just negative all the time it will be impossible for you to move on. Take the proper amount of time to grieve, but remember that your partner and you will most likely have another opportunity to have a family and fulfill that dream again. I truly know that keeping the hope alive will help heal the wounds. Just a note though; thinking about the future is very different than planning every step out. I would highly recommend that you and your partner do not set dates, guidelines, etc. as to when you might try to get pregnant again since it can be an extremely scary thing to think about and the stress level will be high. Also, listen to your wife and see if she wants to try again as the prospect of losing another child may be too much for her to bear. If she does not want to try again right away, or at all, do not make her feel bad or guilty for that. Her feelings are incredibly valid and you need to respect them. If there is no more trying for children, focus on your lives together such as career goals, travel plans, etc. You and her are on this journey together and it is important to be on the same page.

RESPECT HER STRENGTH

While I was writing this book I got nervous that my tips and advice would come off in a very sexist way. In no way do I want it to appear that my wife is, or that I feel she is, weak, fragile or unable to make it without me in any way. I have grown up with strong female role models and I do not want it to appear that I look women as being weaker than men. This book talks about being a support system, a rock, for the mother because this is such a traumatic event that happened to her. Words cannot express the pain felt, nor can we as the man understand so these are ways that we can help. It is important that you never forgot how strong your partner is. She is going through extreme physical and chemical changes and it has been described to me that she is losing a little part of herself. That is an unimaginable amount of pain and suffering that she has to endure. Stephanie has continuously impressed me with how strong she is throughout our relationship but especially during this time. She is a powerful, independent women who doesn't need my help to service but she really does appreciate me and what I do for her. So remember to look at your partner as someone strong who is just going through a daunting experience instead of a weak person who needs you to get through. Also encourage her to go be with friends and family as they can be a really good support system for her as well. I know Stephanie would have her girlfriends over to the house and I would stay in a would have some privacy to talk and be alone and talk. She would also go over to her parents' house and just spend time with them alone. If that is something that your partner does do not be worried that she is tired of you, or that she doesn't want to be around you. It is just another set of tools that she is utilizing in order to heal. Giving her space is important if she needs it. Remember, your partner does not need you to baby her, she is powerful and it is important to embrace that so she can use all the tools at her disposal for healing.

COMMUNICATION IS KEY

One of the very best tips that I was given as Stephanie and I were going through our miscarriage is for me to keep communicating with her. After giving her time to focus solely on her needs and well-being we would talk and share and that brought us closer together. It was an incredibly intimate time to sit and share how I was feeling and it did make me nervous. A lot of you who are reading this may not be the most open or the most vocal when it comes to sharing feelings but it is important for your partner to know and understand you and how you are doing. The worst thing that you can do is to just say that you are "fine" or that everything is "ok". It would be easy for your wife, or anyone, to feel like the miscarriage is not affecting you at all if you don't show it or tell her about how it is. You can be her rock while also being open with her as it will create both a better understanding of what is happening along with a deeper level of trust. If this step makes you nervous, then it may be easier at first to talk to a parent, sibling or friend about your feelings after the miscarriage than it is to speak with your partner. I know that I talked to my parents about how I was feeling during this experience and that helped me vocalize my thoughts to Stephanie. I would suggest that you use the advice that you are given from those sources and then speak with your partner. Try to remind yourself that she is in this with you and that you are in no way alone. If the pain is too great and you or her are having trouble moving on then it might be a good idea to try counseling or therapy. You would be able to see a therapist or counselor alone or with the mother. This will give you a good outlet to get feelings out in a safe environment and it will also give you tools to process these feelings and emotions that you have. There is no shame or embarrassment that comes from turning to a professional when you need it. It does not make you less of a man and it can really help. Remember, it is very important to keep the lines of communication open between you and your partner so you can work on getting through this experience together.

PARTING MESSAGE

This is going to be one of the hardest things that you and your partner will ever go through. The mother will go through immense physical and emotional pain that us men cannot begin to fully understand. We are here to be the Mothers main support system in the journey to get through this event and that may take a lot of time and effort. You have to focus on her needs. Be her rock and her support system that she can turn to whenever she needs it. Take away the different stresses that will only cause her more headaches. Don't forget about yourself though so you can heal from this experience as well. Remember that your partner is a strong, powerful woman who is just going through a tough situation and do not pity or baby her. Lastly, keep the lines of communication open at all times. You are in this together and not being open will create resentment and hurt feelings from all parties involved. Remember that the tips in this book are to be used as a guide, and each person is different so certain tips may not apply to or work for them. I know how tough this is on you, but you and your partner will get through this. I'm sure of it.

ABOUT THE AUTHOR

Erik Fowler is currently finishing his undergrad education at the University of Illinois Springfield and works as an Auditor in Quincy, IL where he lives with his wife Stephanie and their spoiled bichon-poodle Sophie. You can contact him at erikfowlerbooks@gmail.com.

Made in the USA
Lexington, KY
10 January 2018